W9-ATR-284

Wild and Wacky
60 One-Minute Monologues
for Kids

A Smith and Kraus Book
Published by Smith and Kraus, Inc.
177 Lyme Road, Hanover, NH 03755
www.smithkraus.com

Copyright ©2002 by L.E. McCullough
All rights reserved
Manufactured in the United States of America

First Edition: February 2002
10 9 8 7 6 5 4 3 2 1

LIMITED REPRODUCTION PERMISSION:
The publisher grants permission to individual teachers
to reproduce the scripts as needed for use with their own students.
Permission for reproduction for an entire school district
or for commercial use is required. Please call Smith and Kraus, Inc.
at (603) 643-6431.

*Cover and Text Design by
Julia Hill Gignoux, Freedom Hill Design*

Library of Congress Cataloguing-in-Publication Data
McCullough, L. E.
Wild and wacky characters for kids : 60 one-minute monologues / by
L.E. McCullough. —1st ed.
p. cm. — (Young actors series)
Summary: A collection of monologues which focus on power,
personality, and fantasy, aimed at easing childing into the basics
of acting. Includes basic stage directions.
ISBN 1-57525-305-4
1. Monologues—Juvenile literature. 2. Acting—Juvenile literature.
[1. Monologues. 2. Acting.] I. Title. II. Young actor series.
PN2080 .M297 2001
812'.54—dc21
200104957

Wild and Wacky

60 One-Minute Monologues
for Kids

L.E. McCullough

YOUNG ACTORS SERIES

A Smith and Kraus Book

LIBRARY
FRANKLIN PIERCE COLLEGE
RINDGE, NH 03461

ACKNOWLEDGMENTS

My parents, Ervin and Isabel McCullough, who gave me the gift of reading and more love than most children get in several life times. And to as many kid pals I can remember from Cadillac Drive and Arundel Lane, who in many ways helped foster my lifelong predilection to story telling and whimsy: Steve Parshall, Chris Bigelow, Eddie Cowan, Angelo Poulous, Johnny Higdon, Mark Renie, the Noel kids, Tom Leary, Dale Hancock, the Paetz Brothers, the Swinford Sisters, Mike McMillan (R.I.P.), Patty Helvey and her sister Mary, whose "invisible ink" trick was a real "eye-opener." Plus all my Horvay, Manion, Painter, and McCullough cousins. And always Jeff Chiplis who never will grow up and — if this is any kind of a just and sane world — never should.

DEDICATION

To my wife, Lisa Bansavage,
the True Muse of my wandering soul.

Contents

Foreword

Youth of delight, come hither,
And see the opening morn,
Image of truth new-born.
> *William Blake,* Voice of the Ancient Bard

I like nonsense, it wakes up the brain cells.
Fantasy is a necessary ingredient in living.
> *Theodor Seuss Geisel, a.k.a. Dr. Seuss*

Children are natural storytellers. What they experience, what they learn, what they feel each and every day during their ascent from infancy to adulthood is frequently expressed in the form of stories or anecdotes they hear from friends and family. And that's exactly what happens in a good monologue. A character learns or conveys an important bit of information — a sudden comprehension, perhaps, or even wisdom of a kind — about himself and his world.

More children are acquiring an interest in theatre at an ever earlier age. And more elementary school teachers are discovering the value of drama in teaching basic curricula. This book is designed to assist both specialists and non-specialists help their students ease into the basics of acting. For children just starting in theatre, the monologue is the simplest way to instantly become an "actor" with lines that captivate an audience and culminate in an emotional punchline or resolution

For those children who will continue in theatre, the monologue is a crucial foundation for an actor's development. A monologue is more than a mere audition piece; it is a means of mastering the very essence of depicting character.

A good monologue is an *effective* monologue, effective in compelling your audience to listen to you and only you, to be caught up and confined totally in the Moment of You. And yet at the same time to be transported beyond you to other people, other places, other times. Maybe even transported somewhere deep inside themselves . . . a place they might seldom venture, or thought they'd forgotten, or wondered if they'd ever reach.

The key to unlocking the character in a monologue? *Language.* Each one of us on this planet uses language in a distinctive way that imprints our uniqueness as thinking, sentient beings. The language we choose to relate to the world — and to ourselves — reveals much about who we think we are and who we think we can be. When combined with appropriate gesture and intonation, words allow the character in a monologue to emerge and take shape before your very eyes.

These monologues are suitable for both girls and boys and can easily be altered to fit the actor's individual circumstance. Actors should feel free to change a word or two here and there, if needed, and to adapt a monologue to their gender or home town or personal history or situation. The more *personal* the monologue is to the actor, the more *power* the actor can summon in delivery.

Why? Because power and personality are two things that define a monologue. A good monologue (i.e., a monologue that captures and holds the attention of listeners) is all about *character*, all about crystallizing for just a vital few moments the essence of a character and expressing that essence in a novel, exciting, memorable manner.

Some set-up directions have been provided to enhance the actor's understanding of the situation and event sequence; these can be done in mime, unless you really do have a toothbrush or slinky or puddle handy. But to develop better acting technique, an actor should strive to do the monologue without props. It's a skill that will come in handy when you're at an audition and handed a fresh side that says: "character walks on a tight rope above Grand Canyon carrying a stuffed polka-dot mongoose."

These monologues are marked by a strong element of fantasy, hence the title "Wild and Wacky." Childhood is a time when Imagination rules supreme, and Imagination is the center of Art. As has been demonstrated time and again over the centuries, "fantasy" is often the best way to understand and express the "reality" of our world.

In reading this book, have fun meeting sixty new people and making sixty new friends. Each one of these monologues *is* a child, and they're waiting to talk to you, eager to let you know what's on their minds. Listen, and you'll definitely learn a few things about their world — and yours.

L.E. McCullough
Teach Áthas
Woodbridge, New Jersey

CAT AND MOUSE

I walked into my room last night and saw my cat Cocoa playing with a mouse. Hisss! Mrrrowww! Eeeek! It was terrible! She chased the poor little thing all over the desk. Up and down and down and up, Hisss! Mrrrowww! Eeeek! Hisss! Mrrrowww! Eeeek! till finally — she caught it! Then she got on the Internet and ordered some new cat toys. You see, my cat was playing with a computer mouse! When my dad finds out Cocoa used *his* credit card to order those toys, she's going to be in the dog house!

BUTTERCUP

One day my friend Jamie and I were in a field near my house picking wildflowers. We found a big patch of buttercups. We picked a whole handful of them, and I counted the petals. "Guess what?" I said to Jamie. "All the buttercups have five petals." And just as I put them in our collecting sack, I felt something brush my hand. I thought maybe it was a bug. But when I looked down, there was one little buttercup sticking out above the others — and it had six petals! I think it heard what I said, and it wanted to tell us "No, not me, I have six petals! I'm special! Can't you see how special I am?" and it stretched its little head up extra tall so my hand would feel its stem, and I would see how special it was. Jamie said, "I don't know why that buttercup wanted so much to feel special." But I think everyone in the world wants to feel special some time, even a flower.

THE HAUNTED YO-YO

I think my yo-yo is haunted. Every time I give it a spin, it goes crazy. It tries to mess up the tiles when our family plays Scrabble and my dad is about to win — again. Or it tries to knock the socks off our clothesline after my sister has spent a long time putting them up. Once it tried to open the birdcage and make the parakeet dance. And it always wants to hit my big brother on the head, especially when he is asleep. Today at school it tried to drink from the water fountain the same time as Tommy Jennings. Oooh, that was a mess! But I told my teacher that my yo-yo has a ghost inside it, and she believed me! She said, "It is the ghost of a small child who wanted very badly to get attention without earning it." "Gosh," I asked, "is the ghost stuck inside the yo-yo forever?" And my teacher said, "No. It will leave after its owner has spent every recess the rest of the entire year cleaning erasers." I didn't say anything then, but just between you and me, I bet that crazy ghost stops haunting my yo-yo sooner than that.

SUMMER IN A BOX

(Holding a small box or cassette case.) This is my summer box. That's right. Just before school started last fall, I put my whole summer in this box. Well, so I can carry summer around with me all year! On a cold, dark winter's day, I open the box and let out a bit of sunshine, maybe a little warm breeze, and always a fluffy white cloud or two — and I don't feel so cold anymore. And when I am in a sad mood and feeling a little lonely, I just look inside this box, and I see my friends and all the fun we had last summer. *(Opens box slightly and offers to audience.)* Listen . . . can you hear your favorite summer? You can if you try.

THE TOO TALL BOY

My cousin has a friend who knows a boy whose mom is married to a man who has a nephew that is the tallest boy in the world. This boy grew so tall, his shadow couldn't keep up with him and just fell down around his knees. He grew so tall he had to climb up on a ladder to comb his hair in the morning. Just last week he grew so tall his head grew right up out of his hat, and his mom was really freaked out, and she went into kitchen and came out with a big can of lard and told him, "Quick, son, eat this!" "What's that for, Mom?" said the boy. And she said, "Shortening, son."

CLOUD BANK

(Pointing to sky.) See that? Way up there? The gray thing near the sun that looks like a big mushed-out pillow. It's a cloud bank. That's what my grandpa says. What? What do they keep in a cloud bank? Silly! Everybody knows they keep baby clouds in a cloud bank. Why? So the baby clouds can grow and collect interest. Then, when the baby clouds have become mature — that's a grown-up word that means "grown-up" — the cloud mothers and fathers take their baby clouds out of the cloud bank and send them to cloud school, which is like our school except with no desks or chairs or homework. In cloud school the young clouds learn to make rain and snow and how to shelter birds from airplanes that get too close and how to cover the sun so it never gets too hot. Oh, and they also learn to form themselves into shapes that spell letters when God wants to say something to people on Earth. Now that's something I wish we could learn in our school.

DINGLE-PUFFERS

(Laughs.) Ha-ha-ha! *(Stops.)* No, I wasn't laughing, ma'am. Really, I wasn't. Ha-ha-ha! No, please don't send me to the principal's office! It wasn't me laughing! It was the dingle-puffers! You've never heard of the dingle-puffers? Well, ma'am, just about everybody knows a dingle-puffer is a very small person about the size of your little finger's fingernail. And they live right behind your ear. Which is all right, I guess, except they get kind of bored, so they start peeking out to see what's going on and they get tickled by your hair and it makes them laugh. Sometimes — ha-ha-ha! — very loudly. No, I don't think dingle-puffers like detention. Ha-ha-ha! But they sure like laughing! Ha-ha-ha-ha-ha-ha! Bad dingle-puffers, bad!

SAVE THE MOON

(Pointing at ground.) Quick, get a rake! Or a shovel! Or a broom! Hurry! Don't you see? Look there! The moon fell into the swimming pool! We have to get it out before it drowns! What? *(Looks up.)* Well, sure that's *part* of the moon up in the sky. But there's still a lot of it stuck in the pond. Somebody get a lifeguard! Save the moon! Save the mooooooooon!

ONE SMART SLINKY

My Slinky follows me everywhere. At least, I think it's my Slinky. One day I heard this funny noise, like a lot of little metal feet running really fast and going *woing-woing-woing-woing-WOINGGGGGGGGG!* I looked behind me, and there was the Slinky, shaking and breathing hard like it had run a long way to catch up. It might have been somebody else's Slinky but got lost. Or maybe it didn't want to be with the kid who owned it and decided to follow me instead. You might not think a Slinky would care who it followed around. But if I were a Slinky, I'd want to make sure I had a good owner. An owner who kept me bright and shiny and correctly coiled. An owner who never left me out in the rain to rust. An owner who took time to teach me neat tricks. Like reciting *The Pledge of Allegiance*. And memorizing multiplication tables up to fourteen. And saying "Good morning!" in at least nine different languages. Sure, my Slinky can do all that. Doesn't yours?

WELCOME TO THE FAMOUS PANCAKE MUSEUM

Welcome to the Famous Pancake Museum. This is where famous pancakes and famous pancake makers and eaters throughout the ages are given a place of honor and respect. Pancakes have been very important in world history. Did you know that Julius Caesar was a famous pancake maker? Just before a big battle, the Roman army ran out of flour, and the troops were starving. But Julius saved the day by inventing the Caesar Salad Pancake. Unfortunately, one of his men, Brutus, was allergic to the spicy Italian dressing in the pancake syrup and became very sick. When Brutus got back to Rome, he killed Caesar with a spatula. Then Marc Anthony gave a speech and said "We have come not to praise Caesar, but to bury his yucky pancake recipe." And that's why you won't find Caesar Salad Pancakes anywhere else — only here in the Famous Pancake Museum. Isn't history fun?

I WANT TO BE A DENTIST

I want to be a dentist when I grow up. It would be fun! Exploring deep, dark caves in the center of the earth. Finding lost worlds where giant slimy plaque monsters lurk around every corner — just waiting to jump out and grab your fingers! But you'd be nimble and so very quick, and you'd zap out the cavity zombies with your laser ray and leave row upon row upon clean beautiful row of food-free molars and bicuspids gleaming like the sun! Being a dentist would be like playing a video game with a live tongue on the screen. Only you'd never be sure till the very last minute whether it was friend . . . or foe!

BALLOON BASKETBALL

I invented a new game. It's called Balloon Basketball. It's just like regular basketball, except all the players are in hot-air balloons that drift very slowly around the gym. So when someone shoots the ball at the basket, they have to shoot past the other balloons. There would be more passing the ball and more teamwork since the balloons would be moving verrrrrrryyyyyy slowwwwwwwlyyyyyy and getting bumped all around here and there. I don't think as many points would be scored as regular basketball. And the players wouldn't get as much exercise running up and down the court. But you wouldn't have to be really tall to be really good. And wouldn't it be awesome to watch all the balloons floating around? It would be like playing basketball in your dreams!

SHOW AND TELL

My first day at my new school, I knew my teacher didn't like me. "You have a lot of catching up to do," said Mrs. Anderson. "If you don't work hard, you'll be a very sorry third-grader."

That night, I was really sad. Suddenly, I had an idea and ran to the piano bench and grabbed a pencil and a sheet of music paper.

Next morning for Show and Tell, I walked to the keyboard and sang a song I wrote. It was a slow, pretty melody, with notes falling like a soft, gentle rain. As it played, I sang:

> She never smiles at me
> Even though I really like her
> Days go by without the sunshine
> Breaking through her frowns
>
> So I make this wish
> On every rainbow in the world:
> "Help me show her how I feel
> And find the door that opens up
> Her heart to me!"

I stopped playing, and the class was completely quiet. Mrs. Anderson's face grew red, but she didn't say anything. I was sure I would get sent to the principal.

Instead, Mrs. Anderson hugged me, and the class cheered. From then on, everybody in school liked me. And Mrs. Anderson helped me get a scholarship in a special music program for kids.

I used to think piano lessons were a waste of time. Not any more.

THE OCEAN LAUGHING

The best thing I like about going to the beach is standing at the edge of the water with my toes dug in the cool wet sand and feeling the last little wavelet *wusshhing* up over my feet in a big spatter of white foam around my ankles and then dribbling back into the ocean. I stand there and close my eyes and pretend I'm that last little wavelet and I think about where the big ocean takes me every day. Maybe I was on a beach in Japan this morning. Or lapping around the hull of a fishing boat in Mexico. Or maybe floating next to a penguin in Antarctica. Or tickling the toes of some kids on the coast of Morocco and making them laugh and then taking their laughter with me all around the world to share with other kids. *(Cups ear to listen.)* Hear it? It's the ocean, and it's laughing! Laughing along with the fish and the wind and the sea coral and the sun and clouds that make all the weather, until all the laughing becomes a song, a song of joy and wonder about the beautiful planet the ocean makes for us. I think this world would be a better place if more people stood on the beach and listened to the ocean laughing. Don't you?

MARSHMALLOWS ARE THE WAY TO WORLD PEACE

If I were president, people would use marshmallows for money. Marshmallows would be our national currency. That means every time you went to work, you would get paid with a big bag of marshmallows. And every time you needed to buy something, you would pay for it with marshmallows. When you got on a bus or train, you would give the conductor a little string of mini-marshmallows and get a littler string of mini-micro-marshmallows back as change. When you bought groceries or toys or went to a movie or stayed at a motel, you would pay for it with marshmallows. And people would wear big comfy marshmallow packs to carry their marshmallows when they went out, and they would keep their marshmallows in marshmallow banks and buy marshmallow stocks and bonds at the Marshmallow Stock Exchange, and they would only vote for politicians who promised to plant more marshmallow trees in the national parks. And that would stop crime and war. Because you wouldn't need to steal anything except marshmallows, and how many marshmallows can one person have in their house, anyway, before they have to give them away or eat them? And if one country did try and fight a war, how could they have room for their tanks to drive and planes to fly and soldiers to march with all the roads and cities all filled up with marshmallows? If you ask me — and maybe you should — I think marshmallows are the way to world peace.

ANIMALS SLEEPING

I like walking in the woods. Though mostly I don't really walk but find a comfy place to sit. And then I listen. I listen to all the animals sleeping. I can hear them breathing. I can hear their hearts beating. Their eyes fluttering shut. Ssshhh, listen! There's a turtle sleeping nearby, maybe at the end of that log. And over there, some funnel-web spider babies are snoozing in their cocoon inside that tree. Once I came upon a big huge anthill this high all filled with millions of sleeping ants. Ever hear a million ants snoring? Well, it sounds a lot like your grandpa dozing in his easy chair after dinner, only without the burping. Sometimes, if you're really quiet, you can hear some animals dreaming. Ever wonder what a porcupine dreams about? Ssshhh, listen!

POPSICLES IN THE DESERT

(Studiously working calculator.) Hi. I'm figuring how many Popsicle sticks it takes to cover the Sahara Desert. Well, not exactly. I read in the newspaper that the Sahara Desert is the biggest desert in the world — three and a half million square miles. That's a lot of sand. And it's getting bigger every year. That means the people who live there have less land to grow crops and less water to drink. Pretty soon, no one will be able to live there at all. My plan is to make a very large garden hose that the United Nations can use to spray water all over the Sahara Desert and make it come alive again. I can't talk my parents into buying me that much garden hose, but I could use the Popsicle sticks to be a scale model. And who knows? Maybe with the leftover Popsicles we could solve another environmental problem — how to keep the polar ice caps from melting.

THE RIDDLE POLICE

A couple years ago, my family moved into a new town. It was called Riddleville. One day on my way home from school, I was stopped by the police. That's right — the Riddle Police of Riddleville. I was charged with attempting to riddle while walking in a no-riddle zone. They started in on me right away with a barrage of riddles. One false move, and my goose would be toast.

"Tell us, what is red and blue and purple and green? No one can reach it, not a king or a queen?"
"A rainbow in the sky, the last I've seen!"

"What flies forever, rests never and is never caught?"
"The wind, the wind, or so I've always thought."

"What was born when the world was made, but older than a month never grows?"
"The moon up above — why, look how it glows!"

"And how much, how much is the moon above worth?"
"A dollar; it has four quarters, of that I'm sure."

"All right, wiseacre, what has a heart in its head?"
"You must mean lettuce: green, purple or red."

"Then, what has a head but not any hair?"
"A pin or a nail; do you have some to spare?"

"What has a head but cannot think?"
"A match laying on the kitchen sink."

"What has legs but can't walk from here to there?"
"A bed, a table and most likely a chair."

"What passes through a door but never goes in and never comes out?"
"Must be a keyhole you're speaking about."

"What has plenty teeth but cannot eat?"
"A comb or a saw. Tell me, are your questions complete?"

"Officers, this child is sharp as steel! Maybe it's time to riddle him [her] for real?"
"You know, I am starting to get a little bit vexed. I think we'll call my lawyer next."

"And maybe then you can explain why your town's gone mad. I mean, riddles can be fun, but these are really, really bad!"

SHOWER HEAD

Step right up, ladies and gentlemen, and gather round for a look at the greatest invention of the century! It's the new Super Duper Adjustable Power Shower Head! And it's adjustable, did I mention it was adjustable? What? You say you already have an adjustable shower head? Not like this one! The Super Duper Adjustable Power Shower Head has a setting for Sun Shower. All of a sudden a big bright blast of sunshine pours out onto your face! And there's the Snow Shower setting. Zing! You can hear jingle bells all the way to grandma's house! There's a setting for Moon Shower, Star Shower and Meteor Shower — alien spaceships are optional. Of course, my favorite is the Jelly Shower in raspberry, grape and kiwi marmalade. What a great way to start the day! Breakfast in the shower!

MY TALKING TOOTHBRUSH

(Squeezing toothpaste onto a toothrush.) Is that enough? You'd like a little more? No? *(Turns on faucet and puts toothbrush under water.)* Wssshhhhh! Too cold for you? *(Adjusts faucet.)* How is that? Okay, here we go! *(Raises toothbrush to mouth.)* Oh, excuse me. I was just talking to my toothbrush. Well, of course it talks back. Doesn't yours? My toothbrush tells me lots of cool things. Where to brush, naturally, and get all the food particles away from my teeth and gums. And it tells me how good my smile looks. *(Smiles widely.)* Did you know it is impossible to smile on the outside without feeling better on the inside? When you are lonely, a smile is the shortest distance between two people. And you are never fully dressed in the morning unless you are wearing a smile. So you better have a good strong smile ready to go, because all through the day you are going to want to show it to lots of people. *(Cocks ear to toothbrush.)* What was that? Quit talking and start brushing? Okay! *(Brushes vigorously.)*

HELLO. OLA.

Hello. Ola. Aloha. Halo. Hylo. Oi. Hei. Helele. Ni hao. Ei
Je. Ahoj. Salam. Shalom. Ahalan. Bonjour. Bok. Guten Tag.
Salve. Jambo. Molo. Xin chào. Gia'sou. Parev. Zdravo.
Goddag. Hello. That's a friendly sound in every language, don't
you think?

Pronunciation Key: (accented syllable in bold)
  Ola — **o**-la (Spanish)
  Aloha — a-**lo**-ha (Hawaiian)
  Halo — ha-**lo** (Indonesian)
  Hylo — **hy**-lo (Welsh)
  Oi — oy (Portugese)
  Hei — hay (Finnish)
  Helele — hay-**lay**-lay (Sesotho)
  Ni hao — **ni**-how (Mandarin Chinese)
  Ei Je — **a**-jay (Bengali)
  Ahoj — **a**-hoy (Slovak)
  Salam — sa-**lam** (Farsi)
  Shalom — sha-**lom** (Hebrew)
  Ahalan — **a**-he-len (Arabic)
  Bonjour — baw-**zhur** (French)
  Bok — bok (Croatian)
  Guten Tag — goo-ten **tag** (German)
  Salve — **sal**-vay (Italian)
  Jambo — **jam**-bo (Swahili)
  Molo — **mo**-lo (Xhosa)
  Xin chào — **sin**-chow (Vietnamese)
  Gia'sou — **ya**-soo (Greek)
  Parev — pa-**rev** (Armenian)
  Zdravo — iz-**dra**-vo (Serbian, Bosnian)
  Goddag — go-**day** (Danish)

SHIP IN A BOTTLE

(Gazing around at the distant horizon.) Wow! I'm on a ship! An old wooden clipper ship with wide white sails, and we're sailing in a big blue ocean filled with . . . pink bubbles! Pink soap bubbles far as the eye can see! That's because the ship is in a bottle. And the bottle is in a bathtub. Wonder how I got here? Wonder where we're sailing to! Wonder if this bathtub is on a ship that's in a bottle that's in another bathtub? *(Crouches.)* Look out! It's a sea monster! A fifty-foothigh yellow duck, and it's coming toward us! Man the life boats! Trim the mainsail! Anchors aweigh!

UNSOLVED NURSERY RHYMES

So you think nursery rhymes are just innocent kiddie tales, eh? Well, I call them "unsolved mysteries" from Fairy Land. Just what made Georgie "Porgy"? Peter Piper put a lot of effort into picking pickled peppers. Why? How did the cradle that rocked get up on the treetop in the first place? Why didn't the black sheep have a bag for the little boy who cried in the lane? Was he allergic to wool? Personally, I think Miss Muffet was more scared of the curds and whey her mom packed for lunch than any old spider. And Little Boy Blue blowing his horn all the time — that's probably what made Jack and Jill fall down the hill and knock Humpty Dumpty off the wall right into the old woman who lived in a shoe and had so many children she couldn't get them all into the car to go shopping for a bigger shoe to live in.

HOW ABOUT MAUVE?

(Holding hand over eye, turning knob as if on a television, repeating.) I'm adjusting the tint on the world. Everything today is looking a bit too green. Yesterday everything was too grey. So I'm going to make it more, hmmm . . . let's see, how about mauve? *(Turns knob.)* Hold on. Excellent! The world is now officially mauve! Hmmm. I wonder, how do you *think* mauve? Or *feel* mauve? Or *talk* mauve? Uh-oh, something's wrong. *(Hand over eye.)* All the lilacs look brown now. *(Turns knob.)* And the purple people-eaters are becoming yellow yam-snackers. And my friend Violet has turned into my friend Rose! *(Turns knob.)* Oh, no! What have I done!?! I've destroyed the tint balance of the entire world!

WHEN YOU WISH UPON A STAR

(Sings.) "When you wish upon a star." Don't you just love that song? I wonder what it would be like to actually *be* on a star. To exist as a tiny particle of matter way out in space. Since stars are made up of burning gas you'd have to be something lighter than gas, some kind of cloud, maybe. That would be cool! Because if you were a cloud, you could float anywhere. All through the universe! And then you'd look down at kids here on Earth, and you could see them making their wishes, and you could maybe even hear the wishes, too. And maybe — if you were really way-way-way out there in the universe — you would have met God or at least some friendly angels who could help you make somebody's wish here on Earth come true.

OPEN, SAYS ME

(Dramatically.) "Open, Sesame!" Did you ever wonder how the robbers in *Arabian Nights* chose the words that opened their treasure cave? I mean, why "Sesame"? Why not "Open, Spaghetti!!"? Or "Open, Corn Dog!"? Or "Open, Falafel!"? Why did they choose a food word, anyway? Wouldn't it have been simpler to say "Open, Large Underground Rock Deposit in the Middle of the Sandy Desert!"? *(Pause.)* Maybe not. But if I'd been the robber in charge of the cave door code, I would have picked something a little tougher to crack. Something like "Opennnnnnn, You Goshdarned Useless Yoww-Roww-Argle-Bargle-Grumble-Yabba-Dabba-Nogood-Lousy-Piece-of-Dime-Store-Junk!" That's what my dad says when our garage door opener doesn't work. It always seems to open after that.

INVENTIONS 'R' ME

I am going to invent the world's first Fur-Lined Cocoa Cup. Not only would it keep your cocoa warm, it would smell good, too. Mmmm, hot furry cocoa! And to replace the fly swatter — which leaves lots of mushed-up fly guts on everything and is certainly no fun for flies — I am going to invent a Fly Rocket that grabs the fly at one end then shoots it out the other end into insect outer space. I think a Microwave Hair Cutter would be awesome! You would stick your head inside and set the dial for how much you wanted cut, and it would fry off the right amount and leave the ends nice and crisp. Of course, a great inventor always makes use of current technology to improve life as we know it. Do you see all the phone wires going around the city from building to building? Why not turn them into Pizza Runners? When your pizza order is ready, they send it out on the wires straight to your house! And the electricity in the wires keeps the pizza warm, naturally. I may also invent a Used Chewing Gum Flavor Replacer, a Grapefruit-Eating Shield, a Parakeet Diaper and an Electric Grass Clipper you can attach to your feet and walk around the yard clipping grass and reading at the same time. And I am very definitely going to invent a machine that automatically makes your bed. You just push a button and everything folds up like it was before you slept, including your dreams — especially your dreams about inventing things.

HAPPY WILDEBEEST DAY

I like Groundhog Day. If the groundhog sees its shadow, we get six more weeks of cold weather, and that is useful to know. But why should the groundhog be the only animal to get its own day? Every day should be a day to celebrate animals and their role in our daily life. For example, we could have Monkey Day. If the monkey eats five or more peanuts at high noon, it means the circus is coming to town and your parents *will* take you! On Wildebeest Day, if the wildebeest stands on its hind legs, looks up at the sky and gives a sharp squealing bark, it means a large group of hungry lions is nearby and everyone should hide very quickly. You could have Stork Day. If the stork flaps its left wing, your town will have more girls than boys born this year. If the right wing flaps, it means the stork's feathers are too tight, and its elbow itches. And what about Snail Day? If a snail crawls in a straight line for two inches, it means a new French restaurant is going to open up in your neighborhood. If it doesn't move at all, that means it probably got squished. Oops!

DRIVE-BY

When it snowed yesterday, my cousin and I went down to the river where we used to take old pieces of cardboard and pretend they were sleds and then tumble down the bank — fuel-injected, dual-quad Abominable Snowmen at the Indy 500 — neck and neck in the final lap roaring out of the fourth turn, straining for that checkered flag before heading home to Grandma's grilled cheese and cocoa.

Yesterday while we were watching the snow quiet down the afternoon city noise like a soft white blanket over a box of yelping pups, we saw a pack of little boys on fancy painted brandname sleds racing down the bank and yelling and throwing snowballs at each other. Then we saw one of their other little boy buddies come over with his new sled and jump up and holler out so loud you thought he was gonna fall over:

> "Drive-by shooting!
>> Drive-by shooting!
>>> I love this game!
>>>> Lemme play!
>>>>> Lemme play!
>>>>>> Lemme play!
>>>>>>> Lemme play!"

THINGS I WONDER

We live in a very strange and confusing world. For example, do you ever wonder why scientists don't measure the speed of dark? Do you ever wonder why you never see any fleas for sale at a flea market? Or why it is always the last key on the ring that opens the door? Or if the temperature today is zero degrees, and it's supposed to be twice as cold tomorrow, how cold is two times zero going to be? I wonder if a cow laughed, would milk come out her nose? Or if they will ever make mouse-flavored cat food? Or if cannibals don't like to eat clowns because they taste funny? Or if you can catch a criminal by their toeprints? Or why you never grow taller than your head? Or why a person with a narrow mind usually has a wide mouth? Or why most accidents happen accidentally? Mostly I wonder why I think about stuff like this — or am I just thinking I think? I wonder . . .

EVERY TIME I LOSE, I WIN

(Running up huffing, puffing breathlessly.) Wow! That was an awesome race! I was ahead halfway through, then, I don't know what happened — she passed me and I just couldn't catch up. I better go congratulate her. Well, sure, I always congratulate whoever wins. Don't you? I mean, if you won every race, winning wouldn't be special, would it? Besides, there are a lot worse things than losing a race. Like not trying. And every time I lose a race, it reminds me how fun it is to win.

FAUCET MONSTERS

You've got a monster under your bed! Ha-ha-ha! That's crazy! Ha-ha-ha! That's the silliest thing I ever heard, monster under your bed! Ha-ha-ha! Everybody knows they hide in the bathroom faucet. It's a fact! Monsters stopped hiding under kids' beds years ago. A lot of them were allergic to dust and didn't like the fuzz that fell off blankets and got way tired of sharing their space with old shoes and lost toys, so they got into the water pipes all through the house, and that's where they hide. Waiting. Waiting for you to turn the tap to get a glass of water. Or worse, waiting for when you wash your face late at night. *(Mimes washing.)* Waiting for you to lean down over the sink, with your nose just millimeters from the faucet and your eyes full of soap and your hands raised and cupped to catch the water and bring it to your face but all of a sudden you hear a big SNAR-RRRGGG! and a monster pops out of the faucet into your hands and jumps right into your face AAAAUUU-UGGGGHHHH!!!! *(Pause.)* Ooohhh . . . I think I liked it better when monsters lived under the bed. Maybe we can get them to meet us halfway and move into the clothes hamper.

SWIM, SWIM HOME

Last summer I was at the seashore on vaction. Just before dawn I woke up because I was having a terrible dream. I was dreaming that some animal needed water, needed water so bad it was going to die. Right away I thought about my dog Snapper and my cat Tuffy. I begged my parents to call home and check if Snapper and Tuffy were okay. They did call home, and my pets were okay. But I couldn't sleep, so I got up and walked to the beach. The sun was just rising, and that is usually the best time to walk on the beach because it is not crowded yet. But when I got there, a whole bunch of people were standing around, pointing at something in the sand. I went closer and there was a big fish lying in the sand. It had gotten stranded on the beach during the night, and its fins were flapping and its gills were opening up and closing because it couldn't breathe. "That's my animal!" I shouted. "That's my dream animal who needs water!" I picked up the fish and ran down to the water and threw it in! But the waves brought it back to shore. I threw it in again. And again the waves carried it back! So I picked it up again and this time I ran into the ocean, clothes and all, until the water was up to my chest, and I hugged him and heaved him with all my might as far as I could into the water. "Swim, swim home!" I shouted. "Swim home to your family!" And he did.

LOST AND FOUND

(Peering around as if in a big room.) This is an amazing place! It's the Lost and Found Department of my brain! Hey, there's my common sense that Mom always says I'm losing. *(Picks up imaginary object from floor, stuffs it into ear.)* I think I dropped some I.Q. points at the video arcade. Oh, here they are. *(Plucks scattered objects from air, swallows them.)* Good to have those back! Now, if I could only find — whoa, there it is! *(Dashes to other side of stage and stares at floor.)* My natural curiosity! And there's my desire to learn right next to it! Whew! That was a close call. I'd better start wearing earplugs when I sleep so my brains don't leak out. Somebody else might have come here to the Lost and Found and walked off with *my* mind!

HAPPY BUILDINGS

Yesterday, we rode on the train past my dad's old neighborhood where he grew up as a kid. It was full of old buildings. Mile after mile of old, empty, tumble down buildings where nobody lived or worked anymore. Old, tired, grey buildings kneeling by the side of the tracks, falling down a little bit more each day.

My dad didn't say anything, but I could tell he was a little sad. Maybe some of those old buildings still had memories in them. Memories of kids playing in stairwells and families eating dinner together, watching TV or singing to the radio. And I thought if I were mayor of that town, I would take those old buildings and fix them up so kids could play in them again. Make them happy again. Make them stand up again, tall and proud. Make them happy with all the living and laughing and working and playing going on inside them.

Because if we can make more happy buildings in the world, I bet we'll have more happy people.

BURIED TREASURE

(On knees, running hands carefully over ground.) Hi! You may be wondering why I'm out here in the middle of the school soccer field. In the dark. On my hands and knees. With a soup spoon. Well, duhhhhh! I'm digging for buried treasure! *(Digs.)* My history teacher says that before our town was settled, a pirate captain came ashore to hide a chest of silver and gold. The chest has never been found, but I saw an old map in the library, and I think the treasure is buried right under the goalpost. You'll just have to trust me on that, but I've got a lucky feeling! What will I do with the treasure when I find it? Hmmm, you're right . . . if I have to share it with my big brother and sister, I might as well bury it somewhere else. Or take them to the public swimming pool and make them walk the plank!

SHOEHORN

You ever think much about a shoehorn? No, I don't mean a shoe that makes a noise like a trumpet! I mean that little piece of wood or metal or even plastic that you put under your heel to help you slide your foot into a tight pair of shoes. Lots of kids today don't even know what a shoehorn is, probably, since everybody wears sneakers all the time. But a shoehorn is a very neat thing. Cause it's made to do just one job — all the time, every time, forever — and do it in the most simple, most perfect way. Sometimes I wish I were a shoehorn. And had only one thing to do in life. And could do it perfectly all the time, every time, forever.

ELF PRESSURE

(Yawning, rubbing eyes.) Gosh, I had another weird dream! A big giant whale dressed in a Dallas Cowboys football uniform was talking to me about the beet-and-spinach casserole mom served for dinner last night. Yeh, kinda crazy, I know. Soon as the hardware store opens up this morning, I'm going to buy some elf repellent and spray my room before I sleep tonight. Bet you didn't know weird dreams and nightmares were caused by elves sitting on your chest. They figured that out a long time ago in Germany. In fact, the German word for nightmare is "alp-drücken." That means "elf pressure," and sometimes more than one elf sits on you and they squeeze all your body weight up into your brain, which causes the extra pressure that gives you weird dreams and nightmares. It's a scientific fact! I read an article in *Elf Digest!* Anyway, if the hardware store is out of elf spray, I'll ask my parents to put some elf glue on the windowsill to slow them down a bit. I can't take another night of dreaming about beet-and-spinach casserole — especially after I've already had to eat it.

RIP VAN WINKLE

I think one of the coolest stories ever is *Rip Van Winkle* by Washington Irving. This fellow Rip goes bowling in the woods, drinks some magic kool-aid and falls asleep. When he wakes up, it's twenty years later! Wouldn't that be the perfect excuse for missing a math test? Or not cleaning your room or doing chores. "Sorry, Mom, I was asleep for twenty years. Hope somebody fed the cat. Can I have all my allowance, anyway?" If you woke up twenty years from now, you'd be an adult already and would have missed the entire rest of school. Yes! You'd have your driver's license. Yes! And maybe a cool car. Yes! And maybe a family of your own. Whoa! Waaaaaait a minute! You might be married to someone you didn't like. And working a job you hated. And still having to do chores. *And* wanting to sneak off into the woods and fall asleep for twenty years. Just like Rip Van Winkle!

SECONDHAND STORE

My friends and I are doing a play from the 1950s, so we went to a secondhand store to find some old jackets and hats. A secondhand store is where people take old things they don't want any longer — like clothes and furniture and books — so the store can sell them to people who don't have much money to buy new things. It works out for everybody, I guess. We were about to leave when I saw a row of stuffed animals huddled together on a chipped brown shelf. There was a teddy bear with an ear missing and a rabbit with all its fur chewed off. A dog with its big red tongue hanging out and a baby monkey that still smiled even though the person who had owned him had left him there at the second-hand store and wasn't ever coming back. Each one of those animals had their own story. They'd all been loved — sometimes almost to pieces — and then brought there to sit on a dusty shelf, alone now, except for each other. I wanted to say to that monkey, "Come on, buddy, you're coming home with me!" But I didn't. Because I was afraid. Afraid that when I got him home, he would talk to my animals. And tell them about where they were going to live in a few years. And I just thought that's not something they should hear right now.

TOTEM SPINACH

I'm sorry, Mom. I cannot eat the spinach. Spinach is my totem animal. Eating your totem animal is a taboo, a crime against the divine order that can bring misfortune and death. Mom? Mom, stop laughing! I am very serious! You can't go around eating your totem animals and expect to stay healthy! Where did I hear this nonsense? I read it in one of your books from college! A totem animal is an animal who protects you. From what? Well, from my science teacher giving us too much homework. And from forgetting my umbrella on days it rains. And from having to pass the weirdo next door when he walks his invisible cocker spaniel up and down the street. You see, Mom, by not eating spinach, I'm actually living a healthier, happier life. What? Spinach isn't an animal? (chuckles.) Nice try, Mom! Next thing you'll be telling me is hamburgers don't grow on ham trees!

BICYCLE PEOPLE

Our teacher says that there would be less air pollution if more people rode bicycles to work instead of driving cars. I know how there would be even less pollution than that — if people *were* bicycles! Think about if when you were born, you had an operation that fitted wheels onto your legs and gear shifts onto your hands. Then as you grew, you could roll around at the same time you learned to walk. And you wouldn't need a lot of chairs or sofas in your house. You could just lean up against the wall when you wanted to rest. And when you played baseball or football or basketball or any kind of moving sport, you could go really fast because you'd be moving on wheels. Then again, if people were bicycles, you'd have to spend a lot of time cleaning your spokes and oiling your gears. And you'd always have to worry about getting left out in the rain and rusting!

REACH FOR THE STARS

Just because I'm little, people think my dreams don't count. They laugh sometimes, when I tell them I want to be an actor or an astronaut or an architect. And that makes me feel smaller than I already am. So I look up in the sky at the stars that look so small to our eyes but are really about the biggest things in the universe, and I tell myself this poem:

Reach for the stars, they're yours for the taking;
Reach for the stars, someday wonders you'll be making;
Reach for the stars, let them guide you to greatness;
Reach for the stars, and they'll always shine brightly for
   you.

Follow your dream, wherever it leads you;
Follow your dream, let it nourish and feed you;
Follow your dream, never turn from its calling;
Follow your dream, and you'll find your true way in the
   world.

Reach for the stars! Follow your dream!
Reach for the stars! Follow your dream!
Reach for the stars and follow the light of your dream!

IF I WON A MILLION DOLLARS

If I won a million dollars, I would find a home for every stray cat and dog. I would make sure every child got a gift for their birthday. I would plant a tree on every street and a flower in every window. I would paint all the old run-down houses on my block in sunshine colors. I would have fireworks in the sky every night and give every parent a penny to tell their children how much they love them. If I won a million dollars, I would buy harmonicas for every person in the world and hire every music hall to hold harmonica concerts every night and day and fill the world with so much music that pretty soon . . . no one would need to care about money at all.

REALLY MINIATURE GOLF

Last night my friend and I went to a putt-putt golf course. That's where you play miniature golf and try to get the ball past a lot of obstacles. If I owned a putt-putt golf course, I'd make it *really* miniature. I'd have a De-Bigulator Machine that shrank you down to one inch tall, and then you'd play on real-life courses. Like your living room floor in between all the furniture and stuff lying around like shoes and cats and big dustballs. Or a jungle putt-putt out in your backyard, whacking your way past ants and grasshoppers and giant dandelions. Or inside a hamster cage or an aquarium. Or on a birdbath with birds zooming in and out. Or on the kitchen table with plates of food all set out. "Whoops! The mashed potatoes are leaking! It's an avalanche! The gravy is flooding! Run for your life!" Then, when you finished the course, you'd step into the Un-De-Bigulator Machine and come back to normal size.

A SNOWFLAKE AGAIN

Yesterday I was in a cemetery watching my grandmother get buried. It was pretty cold, and I was wearing a warm navy blue coat. It started to snow, the first snow of the winter. I watched the snowflakes fall, not many at first, just floating down from the grey sky like they were leaves falling from trees in autumn. I held out my sleeve, and as the snowflakes landed on my coat, I looked at them. I looked at them really closely and I could see that each snowflake really did have a different pattern. Each snowflake was a special thing that came into the world for a short time and then melted away into the air. And after that, it might become a snowflake again. Or it might become a drop of rain that made a plant grow. Or a molecule of gas that vanished into the sun or even farther into outer space where it might become part of whatever it is that creates the spark of life in the universe, the spark some people call a "soul" and makes each one of us who ever live in this world a unique and completely special person like no one else before or after. So now, whenever it snows, I think of each snowflake being somebody's soul. Travelling to a new life. And being happy to get back out into the universe again. Really, really happy.

A GOOD THUMB
IS A GOOD FRIEND

(Sucking thumb, then pulling it swiftly from mouth and regarding it proudly.) I don't care what anybody says. I'm a thumbsucker and proud of it! Oh, sure, grownups will tell you it's bad for your teeth. And the bullies and smarty-pants in your life will try to make you feel dweebish. But I say this to them — *(Sucks thumb, pops it out with a flourish.)* your thumb is your best friend in the whole wide world! For one thing, you always know where to find it. It's never going to just wander away from you or be on vacation. It's never going to talk about you behind your back. Or break your toys or grab the last piece of candy in the bowl, the candy *you've* been wanting all day! Nope, a good thumb is a good friend. And I've got two of them! *(Sticks both thumbs in mouth.)*

THE OTHER SIDE OF A PUDDLE

(Walking slowly around something on the ground, then stopping.) No, I'm not afraid of getting wet. I know it's only a puddle. But did you ever look at a puddle? Really look *inside* the puddle? Sure, you see your reflection. But what's underneath? Go ahead, look deeper. What's on the other end of a puddle? Do you have the guts to find out? Maybe it's another world, a world that's like ours, only backwards and upside-down, and your name wouldn't be Emily but Ylime, or Mit instead of Tim. Maybe your cat would bark and your dog would climb trees and chase mice. And maybe kids would be grownups and getting gray and going bald, and grownups would be wearing diapers and singing nursery rhymes and riding tricycles while kids drove big cars and trucks. *(Backs up a step and points to ground.)* Who really knows what's on the other side of a puddle? Do you have the guts to find out?

AMBER DAY

You'd better watch out what you say today — *especially* today. Why? Because today is an Amber Day. If you make a false wish on an Amber Day, it will come true. We had some neighbors once, Mr. and Mrs. Poole. They were just the arguing-est pair of folks you ever did see. One day Mrs. Poole was trying to clean house, and she says to Mr. Poole, "Why, you're always in the way! Always clumping around like an old mule! Why, you're nothing but a mule from the waist down!" And he says to her, "Stop yammering, woman! The way you're always braying at people, why you're nothing but a mule from the neck up!" And what do you think but she says back to him: "Eee-yaw! Eee-yaw!" He looks at her, and she's got the head of a mule sitting on her shoulders! And she points to his feet, and he looks down and sees four big mule legs! They'd both been turned into half-mules because of their false wishes on Amber Day! "Eee-yaw! Eee-yaw!" Of course, there's a lot more to the story, but I can't tell you now. I've got to hurry and get some sticky paper to hang on the ceiling for my little sister. She said she wished she were a fly on the wall and, well . . . that's Amber Day for you!

EVEN-STEVEN

(Flipping a coin in the air.) My dad says I don't know how to handle money. He was giving me four quarters a day to take to school. So at recess yesterday this older kid came up to me and said, "Hey! Let me borrow a dollar, but just give me fifty cents." Now that sounded like a good deal to me! So I asked him, "Why should I loan you a dollar but give you only fifty cents?" And he said, "Beause then you will owe me the other fifty cents, and I will owe you the fifty cents you loaned me, and we will be even-steven." Well, that made sense to me, I mean, fifty cents plus fifty cents is one hundred cents, which is one dollar, right? I don't know why my dad thinks I don't know how to handle money. Say, would you like to borrow a three-dollar bill?

AND THEN I WAKE UP

Did you ever look at your cat when it was sleeping? It sleeps soooo peacefully all curled up and dreaming. Dreaming of what? What if your cat was dreaming of you, and your whole life was only a dream in the mind of a cat? It could happen! And it would be pretty cool! But if your life was just a dream in somebody else's sleep, who would you want to be dreaming it? Would you want to be a grownup's dream? Or a kid's dream? The dream of a movie star or a president? Would you want your dreamer to be a person or an animal? What kind of animal? Or are all the animals you know just part of this dream you're in, and in the Real World of the Dreamer there isn't any such thing as a zebra or hippopotamus, and the color blue is really green or there aren't any colors at all, because that's just what your dreamer is dreaming for you. Hmmm . . . I don't know. Somehow I think all that is a little bit more than my cat Smokey has room for in his little cat brain. And then . . . I wake up! Or do I?

HOW TIME FLIES

What if time was longer? What if an hour was seventy minutes and a minute ninety seconds? And a day had thirty hours in it, and a month had forty days and a year fifteen months? What if time not only stretched out but also got slower? Would it take longerrr forrrr youuu toooooo sayyyyyyyy sommmmmethingggggg . . . nggg? *(Lifts arm through air very slowly.)* Orrrrr moooooooove yourrrrrrrrr arrrrrrrr-ummm-ummm-ummm-ummm-ummm-ummm . . . ummm? It might be nice to have things slow down a little bit, last a little longer. Especially summer and weekends! And when you ate a candy bar, it could last way longer. But if time got too long, think how long it would be between birthdays! And you wouldn't be done with school until you were eighty-seven years old! Aaaahhh!

COWABUNGA CATERPILLAR

I saw a man walking down the beach yesterday carrying a surfboard. I noticed that on the end of the surfboard was a caterpillar. I had never seen a caterpillar on a surfboard before. And I thought, that is very interesting. I bet that caterpillar had always wanted to be a surfer. But all of her caterpillar friends had told her, "You are crazy! Caterpillars don't surf!" And the caterpillar asked why, and they told her all kinds of reasons like, "It's too dangerous! It's wrong! It looks silly! It's not something a good caterpillar does!" But she really wanted to surf, whether it was something caterpillars had ever done before or not. And so she found that surfboard and climbed on it and waited until a man picked it up, headed for the ocean to surf. Anyway, that's what I thought when I saw a man walking down the beach yesterday carrying a surfboard with a caterpillar on it. I mean, why else would it be there?

MY FAVORITE BUNYIP

(Casting fishing rod.) I like to go fishing. I'm a good fisher, too. But, between you and me and the yum-yum tree, I get a little help. See those tiny ripples? That's the Bunyip. The Bunyip is a very little person that lives in the stream and helps people catch fish. The Bunyip gets the fish's attention by singing a song and doing a little water dance. The fish sees the Bunyip and thinks, "What in the world is a very little human doing in the water dancing like an idiot and singing a ridiculous song about goober peas? I think I'll eat this thing!" But by then the ripples in the water show where the fish is, and you can catch it — just like that! *(Yanks fishing rod up.)* How do you get a Bunyip to help you fish? Well, my Bunyip actually belongs to my uncle. He's letting me borrow it for awhile. Until I learn to catch a fish of my own.

WISH LIST

All right, everybody, here's the official way to get lots of good luck into your life right *now*. Lock the little fingers of your hands together and turn your thumbs out and up like this! *(Shows hand position.)* Then recite these magic verses:

> Wish, wish on something blue,
> Wish, again to make it true.
> Wish upon a grain of rice,
> Wish and it will turn out nice.
>
> Walk backwards, forwards, circle west,
> Then fold your hands upon your chest.
> Always wish when eating cheese,
> And just before you start to sneeze.
>
> Wish at sunset, noon and dawn,
> Wish on peaches, pears and prawns.
> When you eat a piece of pie,
> Point your fork up to the sky.

And run up to a mailbox and shout, "Johnnie Longlegs ate my corn flakes!"

You'll get your wish. Or have so much fun trying, you won't care if you do or not!

WALKING IN THE CEMETERY

I like walking in the cemetery. You see lots of interesting artwork on the stones. And there is a lot of history you can learn about your community. Am I afraid? Of what? Ghosts? Come on! If dead people's souls do hang around, they probably just want to relax and take it easy. After all, most of them had a tough life and they're pretty tired. Probably they would enjoy hearing about what's going on in their town these days. Somebody who lived in the 1800s would like to know about computers and space rockets, I bet. And people who died from diseases like typhoid and smallpox would be interested in all the new medical cures coming out in our time. Mostly, I think ghosts in a cemetery like to talk to somebody new. I mean, wouldn't you get a little bored if you were stuck in the ground with the same bunch of souls for eternity?

CAPTAIN ANTONYM

"Goodbye, Amy, that dress is very ugly. Would you hate to be enemies? We can leave outside. The library is noisy and warm." *(Pause.)* I am Captain Antonym! I speak only in antonyms — words that mean the opposite from each other. So, what I really just said was: "Hello, Amy, that dress is very pretty. Would you like to be friends? We can go inside. The library is quiet and cool." What? I should say what I mean and mean what I say? Well, that's no fun! Talking in antonyms makes you use your brain to the max. But, if there are those of you out there who dwell in the, shall we say, "slower mental latitudes," I can instantly become — *ta-da!* Captain Synonym! Who is very truly sorry-contrite-regretful-ashamed-embarrassed-apologetic-mortified *and* conscience-stricken to have forced you to exceed your registered brain capacity.

INVISIBLE FRIENDS

Sure I have Invisible Friends. Don't you? Well, I suppose I could loan you one or two of mine. Who would you like? There is Earl King, sort of a small fellow. He speaks German and is a very good guide for walking through the woods. And there is the Elebunicken — a very rare animal that is part elephant, part rabbit, part chicken. It eats lettuce and peanuts and can fly over your head and keep you shady when the sun's really hot. Or you could borrow Millard Fillmore. He was the thirteenth President of the United States. You can ask him what a Whig was and why he doesn't wear one. Invisible friends are great, especially when you move to a new city like my family does every year. You may not be able to take your visible friends with you. But your invisible friends are always there wherever you go.

MAGIC IS AS MAGIC DOES

(Twirling flashlight.) Hi. No, I don't mind you telling me I'm stupid for carrying this old flashlight in the daytime. I don't mind at all. Go ahead and laugh all you want. My *jinni* lives in the flashlight, and I never know when I might need him. You know, a *jinni* — the magical creature that comes out of a lamp when you rub it and gives you three wishes. Well, my *jinni* prefers electricity to kerosene, so it lives in this flashlight. Have I ever used my three wishes? Nope. They're right here in this flashlight, all saved up and ready to go. Would you like a wish? Well, you could have all three, I'm a generous person. Sure, my *jinni* wouldn't mind if you borrowed him for a while. Umm, he does need to have his special *jinni* food. I send away for it, and it's only twenty dollars a box. Yes, if you gave me twenty dollars right now, I'd buy the *jinni* food while you made your wishes. Sure, I'll meet you later. In the park right by the sucker — I mean — honeysuckle tree. *(Takes bill, waves goodbye, smiles.)* So long! Happy wishing!

A GOOD MIRACLE TAKES
A LOT OF PRACTICE*

My grandpa gave me a harmonica when I was six years old, and he taught me how to play it. When I found out he was sick, I made a deal with God that if I learned how to play *Amazing Grace* note-for-note perfect, Gramps would be cured. It would be a miracle, and I would earn it all by myself.

One day I finally did it. Sitting in my room after school, I played *Amazing Grace* note-for-note perfect! I could hardly wait to show Gramps. Just then, Mom's car rolled up in the driveway. I rushed to the door and flung it wide open, ready to hug her and shout out my musical triumph. But I stopped when I saw the sadness in her face.

"Matt . . ." She didn't say anything more for several seconds, and my name just hung there in the cold air. Finally, she spoke. "Gramps died this afternoon."

"No!" I screamed, tears of rage filling my eyes. "It's not *fair!* I prayed and did extra chores and practiced the stupid harmonica till my lips fell off, and and and — *aaahh-hhh!*" Still holding my harmonica, I ran down the street, ignoring Mom's calls to come back. I ran and ran, block after block, sobbing and coughing and blinded by tears. When I finally stopped, it was totally dark, and I sat down on a bench. I stared at the harmonica in my hand. "Stupid, stupid thing! I'll show you who's boss!" And I blew into

* This final monologue is a bonus for the adventurous actor. As are the very best monologues, it is essentially a complete short story. See if you can memorize it, as if you were telling a story to a friend.

the instrument with all my breath, honking and wailing and beeping and baying like a wounded animal, wrenching out sounds that were ugly and angry and mean, hurling my breath into the harmonica faster and faster, harder and harder without plan or pause.

"Hey, you! You with the tooty-tooty thing! C'mere!"

The harmonica nearly fell out of my hands. Even before I turned to face the voice, I knew it belonged to Mr. Hannan, the owner of the Elm Street Laundromat. My first impulse was to run, but that would make even more trouble for Mom. Shoving the harmonica in my pants pocket, I walked slowly toward the doorway where the stocky man waited, plump arms folded and left foot vigorously tapping.

"Was that you playin' the harmonica?"

"Yessir, Mr. Hannan. I'm sorry, I didn't—"

"Sorry!" His beefy red face exploded in laughter. "It sounds terrific! My customers love it."

"Matthew!" It was Mom, trotting up flushed and breathless. "I've been looking all over for you. He hasn't caused any trouble, has he, Mr. Hannan?"

"Trouble! Haw-haw-haw! He's a regular showstopper!" He bent down and looked me straight in the eye. "Listen, pal, here's the deal. You come in my Laundromat every day after school and play your harmonica for an hour, and I'll pay you two bucks to entertain the customers. Saturdays, you play an hour before lunch and one after, five bucks the day, flat. How's about it?"

"You mean, like a job?"

"Yeh, I'm offerin' you a job, kid. You're gettin' paid to practice. Haw-haw-haw!"

"Well, gosh, Mr. Hannan, yeh, I guess, if . . ." I looked at Mom.

"That would be wonderful," she smiled. "Thank you so much. Say thank you, Matthew."

"Th-th-thanks, Mr. Hannan."

Mom and I walked home in silence. At our front doorstep, I paused and bowed my head. "I'm sorry I blew up. But I prayed for a miracle. I asked for Gramps to get well, and he didn't."

"But, Matthew, miracles don't fly out of the sky. And they don't always happen just how we think they should. As Gramps used to say, 'A good miracle takes a lot of practice.'"

She squeezed my shoulders and looked right in my eyes. "Son, you've been given a wonderful gift — the gift of music. It's a very special gift for making people happy, helping them forget about their troubles, getting them thinking about how to make the world a better place. You want a miracle? With that little harmonica, Gramps made sure he'd be with you forever. Every time you pick it up he'll be in your thoughts, won't he? And Mr. Hannan paying you money to play at the Laundromat — well now, I'd call *that* pretty much of a miracle, wouldn't you?"

We both laughed, but then a thought struck me, and I frowned. "Mom, one thing still bugs me. I learned to play *Amazing Grace* note-for-note perfect, but Gramps, he never got to hear me."

She gave me a pat on the shoulder and raised her head to the sky. "Oh, I think he heard you," she said. "I think he truly did."

THE AUTHOR

L.E. McCULLOUGH, PH.D. is an educator, playwright, composer and ethnomusicologist whose studies in music and folklore have spanned cultures throughout the world. Dr. McCullough is the former Administrative Director of the Humanities Theatre Group at Indiana University-Purdue University at Indianapolis and current Director of the Children's Playwriting Institute in Woodbridge, New Jersey. Winner of the 1995 Emerging Playwright Award for his stage play *Blues for Miss Buttercup*, he is the author of *The Complete Irish Tinwhistle Tutor*, *Favorite Irish Session Tunes* and *St. Patrick Was a Cajun*, and three highly acclaimed music instruction books. He has performed on the soundtracks for the PBS specials *The West*, *Lewis and Clark* and *Not for Ourselves Alone: The Story of Elizabeth Cady Stanton and Susan B. Anthony*. Since 1991 Dr. McCullough has received 46 awards in 31 national literary competitions and has had 179 poem and short story publications in 91 North American literary journals. He is a member of The Dramatists Guild, American Conference for Irish Studies, Southeastern Theatre Conference and the National Middle School Association. His books for Smith and Kraus include: *Plays of the Songs of Christmas*; *Stories of the Songs of Christmas*; *Ice Babies in Oz: Original Character Monologues*; *Plays of America from American Folklore, Vol. 1 & 2*; *Plays of the Wild West, Vol. 1 & 2*; *Plays from Fairy Tales*; *Plays from Mythology*; *Plays of People at Work*; *Plays of Exploration and Discovery*; *Anyone Can Produce Plays with Kids*; *Plays of Ancient Israel*; *Plays of Israel Reborn*; *Ultimate Audition Book for Teens, Vol. 2*; and *"Now I Get It!": 12 Ten-Minute Classroom Drama Skits for Elementary Science, Math, Language & Social Studies, Vol. 1 & 2*.

Franklin Pierce College Library

00160117

DATE DUE

MAY 2 6 2006 ILL 19654077 HCD

GAYLORD   PRINTED IN U.S.A.